Come Home, My Soul

31 Days of Praying the Living Word

Other books by Stephen A. Macchia:

Becoming A Healthy Church

Becoming A Healthy Church Workbook

Becoming A Healthy Disciple

Becoming A Healthy Disciple: Small Group Study and Worship Guide

Becoming A Healthy Team

Becoming A Healthy Team Exercises

Crafting A Rule of Life

Wellspring: 31 Days to Whole Hearted Living

Path of a Beloved Disciple: 31 Days in the Gospel of John

Broken and Whole: A Leader's Path to Spiritual Transformation

Outstretched Arms of Grace: A 40-Day Lenten Devotional

Legacy: 60 Life Reflections for the Next Generation

Come Home, My Soul

31 Days of
Praying the Living Word

STEPHEN A. MACCHIA

LEADERSHIP
TRANSFORMATIONS INC.

Published by **Leadership Transformations (LTI Publications)**
P.O. Box 338, Lexington, MA 02420
www.leadershiptransformations.org

April 2018

Printed in the United States of America.

Library of Congress Cataloging-in-Publication Data
Macchia, Stephen A., 1956–
Legacy / Stephen A. Macchia.
Includes bibliographical references.

ISBN 978-0-692-11541-1 (pbk.)

Dedicated to

all who teach and practice Sacred Reading
of the Scriptures

Come Home, My Soul

Table of Contents

Introduction 1

Day 1: Hannah 5

Day 2: Jonah 9

Day 3: Nehemiah 14

Day 4: Daniel.. 19

Day 5: David... 24

Day 6: Habakkuk 29

Day 7: Mary.. 33

Day 8: Zechariah and Simeon................................ 37

Jesus and Prayer.. 42

Day 9: The Lord's Prayer 44

Day 10: Jesus' High Priestly Prayer 49

The 7 Last Words of Jesus on the Cross.............. 53

Day 11: Paul's Prayer for Direction 57

Day 12: Paul's Prayer for Unity 61

Day 13: Peter, John and Believers 65

Day 14: Stephen 69

Day 15: Revelation of John (Part 1) 73

Day 16: Revelation of John (Part 2) 77

Day 17: Psalm 1, 19 and 119 81

Day 18: Psalm 8 84

Day 19: Psalm 16 87

Day 20: Psalm 23 91

Day 21: Psalm 25 95

Day 22: Psalm 42 99

Day 23: Psalm 46 103

Day 24: Psalm 55 108

Day 25: Psalm 62 114

Day 26: Psalm 63 119

Day 27: Psalm 84 123

Day 28: Psalm 103 128

Day 29: Psalm 121 132

Day 30: Psalm 139 136

Day 31: Psalm 100, 150.. 142

Come Home, My Soul

Introduction

Dear Friend,

What would it look like for you to join some of your favorite biblical characters in the prayers they once prayed? How would it feel to use these prayers, preserved for us in the Scriptures, as templates for our own soul's refreshment and renewal? Perhaps your soul will feel at home, close to the heart of God, as you sit with these prayers in your own spiritual journey.

For the next month, you are invited into a personal prayer experience that's biblical and reflective. The prayers noted are given to us as examples for how our prayers can be shaped and delivered: straight from the heart. For the first half of the month, we will consider prayers written by key people in the Bible, including our Lord Jesus Christ, who prioritized a life of prayer and has given us the best road map for our own prayers. The second half of the month will feature our most beloved prayer book, the Psalms, from which we see prayers offered with passion and emotion, stemming from the most visceral to the most vibrant.

There is no "right way" to pray. We have freedom to pray in the most natural ways possible, using words that reflect the raw material of our lives. When we are in our prayer closet, God invites us to be present with him. God wants us to share from the depth of our hearts as we attend to his heart. Scripture in particular reveals to us this attentiveness and freedom in prayer. Therefore, when we learn to pray biblically, we are practicing how best to pray from the depth of our souls. Biblical prayers illumine the pathway for our life of prayer. How kind of God to guide us so graciously.

In addition, we might want to consider new ways to pray that others invite us to consider. This might include adding praise to our lips or words of gratitude for the gifts God has so freely given in this life. Perhaps there are people we know who need healing, help, or hope, and our prayers become focused on another. We might cry out in agony or in joy. We might give voice to the longings of our soul. Bottom line: there is no right or wrong way to pray. God hears our hearts, words, tears, adorations, confessions, thanksgivings, and supplications. And, he loves that we want to listen to his voice and respond with our own.

Ponder some of the great prayers of God's people. Give yourself permission to personalize the words. Make them your own prayers too. Moses prayed very simply "If you are pleased with me, teach me your ways so I may know you and continue to find favor with you" (Exodus 33:13). How can you join Moses and pray for God's favor over your own life today? Over the next 31 days, feel free to add your name into the prayer narratives of others like David, Habakkuk, Nehemiah, Hannah, Mary, Paul, and John. Come home to the heart of God through the prayers of his beloved disciples. You will find rest for your soul. Praying the Scriptures in this way will bring health and vitality to your spiritual journey. May this month be filled with the promises of God expressed deeply and authentically in your homeward bound prayers with the Lord.

Your Brother in Christ

Stephen A. Macchia
Lexington, Massachusetts

Come Home, My Soul

Day 1

Hannah

We begin with Hannah, who cried out to God, pleading for a child. Hannah continued to cry out for mercy, even though the Lord had closed her womb. She was married to Elkanah, and to make matters worse, Peninnah (Elkanah's other wife) provoked Hannah. Deep in anguish, Hannah prayed and wept bitterly, vowing to the Lord Almighty, "If you will only look on your servant's misery and remember me, and not forget your servant but give her a son, then I will give him to the Lord for all the days of his life" (1 Samuel 1:11). Eli, the priest of her day, once saw Hannah's lips moving but voicing nothing and misinterpreted her emotional prayer as if she was drunk with wine. Hannah pleaded for his mercy as she poured out her soul to the Lord. Eli blessed Hannah, "Go in peace, and may the God of Israel grant you what you have asked of him" (vs. 17).

God, who knows the hearts of all who love him, chose to grant Hannah's request. In time, she became pregnant and gave birth to her son Samuel, "Because I asked the Lord for him." Bringing her son back to Eli, they worshiped the Lord who granted her what she had asked for. Samuel would later serve alongside Eli and accomplish great things for the Lord. He would be the last judge of Israel and the first of the prophets of Moses. He would ultimately choose and anoint both Saul and David as kings of Israel. God graciously kept the womb of Hannah open and she and Elkanah had three more sons and two daughters.

The following prayer is one of praise for the deliverance and provision granted so generously to this faithful woman of God. As you reflect on this prayer, consider how God has delivered you from your own personal agonies and pray with Hannah these words of praise and adoration. There is no one like our God!

Today...

Join Hannah and give thanks for God's provision (**1 Samuel 2: 1-3**)

My heart rejoices in the Lord;
in the Lord my horn[a] is lifted high.
My mouth boasts over my enemies,
for I delight in your deliverance.
There is no one holy like the Lord;
there is no one besides you;
there is no Rock like our God.
Do not keep talking so proudly
or let your mouth speak such arrogance,
for the Lord is a God who knows,
and by him deeds are weighed.

As you reflect on the Word, how is God inviting you to pray? What biblical words or phrases are you led to use in your own prayer?

_____

_____

_____

_____

_____

_____

_____

_____

_____

_____

_____

_____

_____

Behold the splendor of the Lord – Believe the promises of his love – Belong to those who unreservedly trust him – Become prayerful in all you are and do.

Day 2

Jonah

Jonah's story is familiar to our own. The Lord command-ed him to go to the great city of Ninevah and preach against it because of its wickedness. But Jonah disobeyed the Lord, running away from the Lord and heading in-stead for Tarshish. The Lord knew Jonah was running from him and watched as Jonah found a ship headed to Tarshish and went onboard. The Lord sent a great wind to the sea, causing a violent storm. The sailors were afraid. Each cried to his own god. They threw cargo overboard to lighten the ship. They found Jonah sleeping in the belly of the ship. They cast lots to find out who was responsible for this calamity. The lot fell on Jonah. The sailors threw Jonah into the sea, knowing he was running away from the Lord because of his confession.

At the Lord's provision, Jonah landed in the belly of a huge fish. He was there three days and nights. From in-side the fish, Jonah prayed the prayer below. Then the fish thrusted Jonah out of its belly. Back on dry land, Jonah finally relented and followed God's call to Ninevah, where he preached repentance and the people responded. But Jonah was still dissatisfied with what felt to him as a gross injustice. He said to the Lord, "I knew that you are a gracious and compassionate God, slow to anger and abounding in love." (Jonah 4:2) God permitted his anger despite Jonah's immature response. God's mercy and compassion is unstoppable.

We find it hard to imagine that Jonah's story really happened, but the reality is a wake up call of epic proportions. Why did God allow for this to occur? Was this the only way to get Jonah's attention? How many times do we ignore the commands and precepts of God and choose our own path? When we do, we too may find ourselves in outrageous predicaments. In distress, Jonah calls out to God to relieve him of his desperation and bring much needed change to his trying circumstance. Because of God's mercy and grace, Jonah is eventually released from the belly of the whale and his life is saved. Ultimately, the word, will and ways of God are fulfilled.

Today…

Join Jonah and pray for God's mercy in spite of our rebellious disobedience
(**Jonah 2**)

From inside the fish Jonah prayed to the Lord his God.
He said:
In my distress I called to the Lord,
and he answered me.
From deep in the realm of the dead I called for help,
and you listened to my cry.
You hurled me into the depths,
into the very heart of the seas,
and the currents swirled about me;
all your waves and breakers
swept over me.
I said, 'I have been banished
from your sight;
yet I will look again
toward your holy temple.'
The engulfing waters threatened me,
the deep surrounded me;
seaweed was wrapped around my head.
To the roots of the mountains I sank down;
the earth beneath barred me in forever.
But you, Lord my God,
brought my life up from the pit.
When my life was ebbing away,

I remembered you, Lord,
and my prayer rose to you,
to your holy temple.
Those who cling to worthless idols
turn away from God's love for them.
But I, with shouts of grateful praise,
will sacrifice to you.
What I have vowed I will make good.
I will say, 'Salvation comes from the Lord.'
And the Lord commanded the fish, and it vomited Jonah
onto dry land.

As you reflect on the Word, how is God inviting you to pray? What biblical words or phrases are you led to use in your own prayer?

_____

_____

_____

_____

_____

_____

_____

_____

_____

_____

_____

_____

Behold the splendor of the Lord – Believe the promises of his love – Belong to those who unreservedly trust him – Become prayerful in all you are and do.

Day 3

Nehemiah

Nehemiah is a man after God's heart and a cupbearer of king Artaxerxes. Nehemiah's unique role in the building up of God's Kingdom included the incredible reconstruction of the wall surrounding Jerusalem. Early in the book of Nehemiah, we find him praying for God's mercy and forgiveness, for himself, his family, and his generation. Artaxerxes blesses Nehemiah and a team of high priests and members of each tribe who together rebuild the wall. This truly marvelous accomplishment is made possible by Nehemiah's gifted leadership and the godly team he assembled.

Even before the king permits Nehemiah to begin rebuilding the wall, Nehemiah comes clean before the Lord. He acknowledges with specificity the sin of disobeying God's commandments and the ways God's instructions were not heeded or fulfilled among his and previous generations. Like so many biblical prayers, Nehemiah's prayer features authentic vulnerability and the willingness to acknowledge brokenness and sinfulness in a contrite manner. This is a good word for our own generation. May Nehemiah's prayer inspire you to do likewise.

Today...

Join Nehemiah and pray for God's forgiveness and redemption (**Nehemiah 1:5-11**), in preparation for the fulfillment of his will and ways.

Lord, the God of heaven, the great and awesome God, who keeps his covenant of love with those who love him and keep his commandments, let your ear be attentive and your eyes open to hear the prayer your servant is praying before you day and night for your servants, the people of Israel. I confess the sins we Israelites, including myself and my father's family, have committed against you. We have acted very wickedly toward you. We have not obeyed the commands, decrees and laws you gave your servant Moses.

Remember the instruction you gave your servant Moses, saying, 'If you are unfaithful, I will scatter you among the nations, but if you return to me and obey my commands, then even if your exiled people are at the farthest horizon, I will gather them from there and bring them to the place I have chosen as a dwelling for my Name.'

They are your servants and your people, whom you redeemed by your great strength and your mighty hand. Lord, let your ear be attentive to the prayer of this your servant and to the prayer of your servants who delight in revering your name. Give your servant success today by granting him favor in the presence of this man.

Also note how Nehemiah prays again after completing the wall (**Nehemiah 9**). Consider prayerfully how careful he was to list by name all contributors to the reconstruction efforts. Nehemiah and the people of God dedicated the wall (**Nehemiah 12**) joyfully with songs and thanksgiving and read the Book of Moses.

As you reflect on the Word, how is God inviting you to pray? What biblical words or phrases are you led to use in your own prayer?

_____

_____

_____

_____

_____

_____

_____

_____

_____

_____

_____

_____

_____

Behold the splendor of the Lord – Believe the promises of his love – Belong to those who unreservedly trust him – Become prayerful in all you are and do.

Day 4

Daniel

The prophetic word of Daniel is filled with adoration and admonition. Daniel knows the height, depth, length, and breadth of God's amazing love and responds with praise and worship for God and God alone. But he also recognizes our desperation for God. With full conviction, Daniel recounts the many ways we stumble because of our outright disobedience. His faithful life of service in the Kingdom of God includes the fact that he was from David's lineage, a member of his dynasty and royal family. A good-looking man, Daniel was renowned for his wisdom and intelligence, his righteousness and his ability to interpret dreams. He served in government positions under four kings, his ministry spanning a remarkable 70 years. Daniel is known best for his being thrown into the lion's den, but what many don't realize is that he was most likely in his 80s when this occurs. We don't have any "dirt" on Daniel. Instead he's one of the biblical heroes we turn to who is admirable and righteous.

Once again, Daniel's prayer is filled with straightforward repentance, and that's in spite of Daniel's unparalleled obedience to the Lord in his day. A healthy prayer before our great and awesome God includes not only our praise and petition, but must begin with our confession: admitting our propensity toward sinful self-absorption and our unwillingness to acknowledge the wisdom and word of God. Are you willing to give words to your own sinfulness and in turn cry out for God's abundant mercy, grace, and peace?

Today…

Join Daniel and pray for God's forgiveness and favor (**Daniel 9: 3-19**)

So I turned to the Lord God and pleaded with him in prayer and petition, in fasting, and in sackcloth and ashes.

I prayed to the Lord my God and confessed:

Lord, the great and awesome God, who keeps his covenant of love with those who love him and keep his commandments, we have sinned and done wrong. We have been wicked and have rebelled; we have turned away from your commands and laws. We have not listened to your servants the prophets, who spoke in your name to our kings, our princes and our ancestors, and to all the people of the land.

Lord, you are righteous, but this day we are covered with shame—the people of Judah and the inhabitants of Jerusalem and all Israel, both near and far, in all the countries where you have scattered us because of our unfaithfulness to you. We and our kings, our princes and our ancestors are covered with shame, Lord, because we have sinned against you. The Lord our God is merciful and forgiving, even though we have rebelled against him; we have not obeyed the Lord our God or kept the laws he gave us through his servants the prophets. All Israel has transgressed your law and turned away, refusing to obey you.

Therefore the curses and sworn judgments written in the Law of Moses, the servant of God, have been poured out on us, because we have sinned against you. You have fulfilled the words spoken against us and against our rulers by bringing on us great disaster. Under the whole heaven nothing has ever been done like what has been done to Jerusalem. Just as it is written in the Law of Moses, all this disaster has come on us, yet we have not sought the favor of the Lord our God by turning from our sins and giving attention to your truth. The Lord did not hesitate to bring the disaster on us, for the Lord our God is righteous in everything he does; yet we have not obeyed him.

Now, Lord our God, who brought your people out of Egypt with a mighty hand and who made for yourself a name that endures to this day, we have sinned, we have done wrong. Lord, in keeping with all your righteous acts, turn away your anger and your wrath from Jerusalem, your city, your holy hill. Our sins and the iniquities of our ancestors have made Jerusalem and your people an object of scorn to all those around us.

Now, our God, hear the prayers and petitions of your servant. For your sake, Lord, look with favor on your desolate sanctuary. Give ear, our God, and hear; open your eyes and see the desolation of the city that bears your Name. We do not make requests of you because we are righteous, but because of your great mercy. Lord, listen! Lord, forgive! Lord, hear and act! For your sake, my God, do not delay, because your city and your people bear your Name.

As you reflect on the Word, how is God inviting you to pray? What biblical words or phrases are you led to use in your own prayer?

_____

_____

_____

_____

_____

_____

_____

_____

_____

_____

_____

_____

_____

Behold the splendor of the Lord – Believe the promises of his love – Belong to those who unreservedly trust him – Become prayerful in all you are and do.

Day 5

David

King David was a man after God's heart. Once a shepherd boy tending to the flock in the fields of his father's homestead, God called him to rule over his people. He was a mighty warrior king, faithful to defeat the enemies of God's chosen ones. He was experienced in leadership, coming out of a shepherding heart of love and worship. He ruled well and the people flourished. But he was far from perfect. In 2 Samuel 11, we discover how David fell from grace when lusting for another man's wife became his sole preoccupation. His sin with Bathsheba led him into irrational attempts to hide his adultery. He began by calling Bathsheba's husband Uriah home from battle, assuming he would take advantage of a temptation to return home and lay with his wife. When he refused, David schemed and plotted for faithful Uriah's death. David sent Uriah to fight on the front lines of David's battlefield – a cover-up of epic proportion.

On the heels of his most desperate season of sinfulness and self-deception recorded for us in 2 Samuel 12, with the help of Nathan's confrontational friendship, David finally comes to his senses and with heartbroken acknowledgement of his disobedience before God, he writes some of the most striking words of repentance in the Scriptures. Psalm 51 (in addition to Psalm 32) is the cry of a desperate man's heart, a man who is known to be one of God's abundantly blessed servants. As a shepherd boy, he learned how to lead. As a conqueror of a giant, he discovered the appropriate use of power. As a worshiper, he practiced a life of submission. As a psalmist, he modeled a life of prayer. Now he acknowledges that the greatest expression of authority is by way of his brokenness and vulnerability. In this prayer, remember your own need for God and recall afresh the significance of a life of prayerful repentance… which will ultimately lead you to receive the gifts of hope, peace, and joy in the Lord.

Today…

Join King David in acknowledging your sin(s) before and toward God, and plead for his mercy, cleansing, and grace. Invite joy, gladness, and a steadfast spirit to sustain you, as your broken and contrite heart is joyfully renewed and restored from the inside out. (**Psalm 51**)

Have mercy on me, O God,
according to your unfailing love;
according to your great compassion
blot out my transgressions.
Wash away all my iniquity
and cleanse me from my sin.
For I know my transgressions,
and my sin is always before me.
Against you, you only, have I sinned
and done what is evil in your sight;
so you are proved right in your verdict
and justified when you judge.
Surely I was sinful at birth,
sinful from the time my mother conceived me.
Yet you desired faithfulness even in the womb;
you taught me wisdom in that secret place.
Cleanse me with hyssop, and I will be clean;
wash me, and I will be whiter than snow.
Let me hear joy and gladness;
let the bones you have crushed rejoice.

Hide your face from my sins
and blot out all my iniquity.
Create in me a pure heart, O God,
and renew a steadfast spirit within me.
Do not cast me from your presence
or take your Holy Spirit from me.
Restore to me the joy of your salvation
and grant me a willing spirit, to sustain me…

As you reflect on the Word, how is God inviting you to pray? What biblical words or phrases are you led to use in your own prayer?

_____

_____

_____

_____

_____

_____

_____

_____

_____

_____

_____

_____

_____

_____

_____

Behold the splendor of the Lord – Believe the promises of his love – Belong to those who unreservedly trust him – Become prayerful in all you are and do.

Day 6

~~~

Habakkuk

Habakkuk knew the secret of contentment and joy. His role in the community of faithful prayer warriors is one of transparency and trust amidst undeniably difficult circumstances. His prayer today defines the word "joy" better than many other places. Here he freely articulates what's missing in life – no fig buds, no grapes on the vine, no olives on the trees, no crops in the fields, no sheep in the pen or cattle in the stalls. And yet, he finds room in his heart to rejoice and give thanks – to be glad, content, and full of rejoicing. Habakkuk's testimony is an inspiration to followers of God in every generation.

So often we look at what's missing in our lives. We moan about what we lack. We complain about what's absent from our lives rather than find contentment and peace within the constraints of our lives. We tend to look over the fence and want what belongs to another. We lust for the things of this world more than hunger for the things of God. Our humanity boasts of the material when all the while God is offering us a better way, even if it means suffering, loss, and deprivation of material "blessings" and "things" we have come to believe are formative of our identity.

But in this prayer, we remember with thanksgiving the myriad hidden and intangible gifts all around us, and the abundance offered to us by our generous and loving God. When we can offer our praise to God despite the apparent disheartening situations of our day, God fills our hearts with truly biblical joy.

Today...

Join Habakkuk and pray for God's joy no matter
what comes your way and in spite of what you
feel is missing in your life with God
(**Habakkuk 3: 1-2; 17-19**).

*Lord, I have heard of your fame;
I stand in awe of your deeds, Lord.
Repeat them in our day,
in our time make them known;
in wrath remember mercy...
Though the fig tree does not bud
and there are no grapes on the vines,
though the olive crop fails
and the fields produce no food,
though there are no sheep in the pen
and no cattle in the stalls,
yet I will rejoice in the Lord,
I will be joyful in God my Savior.
The Sovereign Lord is my strength;
he makes my feet like the feet of a deer,
he enables me to tread on the heights.*

As you reflect on the Word, how is God inviting you to pray? What biblical words or phrases are you led to use in your own prayer?

_____

_____

_____

_____

_____

_____

_____

_____

_____

_____

_____

_____

_____

_____

Behold the splendor of the Lord – Believe the promises of his love – Belong to those who unreservedly trust him – Become prayerful in all you are and do.

Day 7

Mary

God selected a young woman to bear the Messiah, Jesus. One can only wonder and imagine what Mary was thinking as God chose her to carry in her womb the Savior of the world. We know an angel pronounced the declaration from heaven. We know she pondered this reality deeply, thoughtfully, and prayerfully. Her soul must have been as full as her pregnant body, enveloped by the grace of God and appropriately overwhelmed as she considered how her life would be transformed by the arrival of her child. Little did Mary know how central her role would become as shepherds and kings, leaders and locals, pilgrims and sojourners, would sit at her Son's feet and witness and worship him with adoration.

As we ponder today's prayer, let's recall how Mary followed her son, Jesus, every step of the way during his earthly life and even to the cross, the tomb, and the resurrection. Hers was a life of gentle, gracious and loving obedience. Hers was a life devoted to following her Lord and Savior, Jesus. Hers was a life of self-effacing self-sacrifice. Hers was a life of prayerful noticing, giving voice to her heart's deepest desires. Hers was a life in harmony with the Spirit of God and in obedience to the Word of God. Hers was a life blanketed by prayerfulness, faithfulness, and loving devotion. May it be so for each of us who claim Jesus' miraculous Incarnation.

Today...

Join Mary and pray for God's grace
(**Luke 1: 46-55**) as you wonder, wait and watch
how God envelops and empowers you with his
loving mercy.

*My soul glorifies the Lord
and my spirit rejoices in God my Savior,
for he has been mindful
of the humble state of his servant.
From now on all generations will call me blessed,
for the Mighty One has done great things for me—
holy is his name.
His mercy extends to those who fear him,
from generation to generation.
He has performed mighty deeds with his arm;
he has scattered those who are proud in their inmost
thoughts.
He has brought down rulers from their thrones
but has lifted up the humble.
He has filled the hungry with good things
but has sent the rich away empty.
He has helped his servant Israel,
remembering to be merciful
to Abraham and his descendants forever,
just as he promised our ancestors.*

As you reflect on the Word, how is God inviting you to pray? What biblical words or phrases are you led to use in your own prayer?

_____

_____

_____

_____

_____

_____

_____

_____

_____

_____

_____

_____

_____

_____

Behold the splendor of the Lord – Believe the promises of his love – Belong to those who unreservedly trust him – Become prayerful in all you are and do.

Day 8

Zechariah and Simeon

Two cousins, Elizabeth and Mary, are great with child. Elizabeth is nearing the birth of her son, John (the Baptist). Mary is close to the miraculous delivery of her son, Jesus. Surrounding these two women are family members and community leaders who are awed by their devotion to God. Zechariah is the husband of Elizabeth, and even though an angel visits him, has a hard time believing the words of the angel and is gripped with fear. The angel tells Zechariah, "Do not be afraid…your prayer has been heard. Your wife Elizabeth will bear you a son, and you are to call him John." Because of his agedness, Zechariah has a hard time believing this to be true and is thereby silenced until John's birth. When Zechariah is able to speak and declare the name of his son, his tongue is loosed with joy, his heart praising the Lord for his redemption and salvation. A wonderful prayer ensues (the first of two prayers today).

An angel also meets Mary, declaring her forthcoming miraculous conception. Mary asks the angel, "How will this be, since I am a virgin?" Unlike Zechariah, she receives this angelic utterance and offers herself to God, "I am the Lord's servant…may your word to me be fulfilled." When Joseph and Mary present Jesus in the temple, the righteous and devout Simeon offers praise to the Lord for the provision of Jesus the Messiah. He had been waiting for the Lord's Messiah under the strength and inspiration of the Holy Spirit. When Joseph and Mary bring Jesus to the temple, as it was customary to do, Simeon takes Jesus in his arms and praises God with absolute delight. His prayerful response is telling: here's a man who was waiting many years for the Messiah and what ensued was the profound peace of God in Christ.

Today...

Join Zechariah and pray for God's redemptive work in your heart (Luke 1: 68-75)

Praise be to the Lord, the God of Israel,
because he has come to his people and redeemed them.
He has raised up a horn of salvation for us
in the house of his servant David
(as he said through his holy prophets of long ago),
salvation from our enemies
and from the hand of all who hate us—
to show mercy to our ancestors
and to remember his holy covenant,
the oath he swore to our father Abraham:
to rescue us from the hand of our enemies,
and to enable us to serve him without fear
in holiness and righteousness before him all our days.

Join Simeon and pray for God's peace (**Luke 2: 25-32**)

Now there was a man in Jerusalem called Simeon, who
was righteous and devout. He was waiting for the consola-
tion of Israel, and the Holy Spirit was on him. It had been
revealed to him by the Holy Spirit that he would not die
before he had seen the Lord's Messiah. Moved by the Spirit,
he went into the temple courts. When the parents brought
in the child Jesus to do for him what the custom of the Law

required, Simeon took him in his arms
and praised God, saying:
Sovereign Lord, as you have promised,
you may now dismiss your servant in peace.
For my eyes have seen your salvation,
which you have prepared in the sight of all nations:
a light for revelation to the Gentiles,
and the glory of your people Israel.

As you reflect on the Word, how is God inviting you to pray? What biblical words or phrases are you led to use in your own prayer?

_____

_____

_____

_____

_____

_____

_____

_____

_____

_____

_____

_____

Behold the splendor of the Lord – Believe the promises of his love – Belong to those who unreservedly trust him – Become prayerful in all you are and do.

Jesus and Prayer

The Bible tells us to "pray without ceasing" (1 Thess. 5:17).

Jesus came closest to this command of any person who has ever lived on this planet. He was continually in a prayer mode:

- alone (Matt. 14:23; Mark 1:35; Luke 9:18; Luke 22:39-41)
- in public (John 11:41-42; 12:27-30)
- before meals (Matt. 26:26; Mark 8:6; Luke 24:30; John 6:11)
- before important decisions (Luke 6:12-13)
- before healing (Mark 7:34-35)
- after healing (Luke 5:16)
- to do the Father's will (Matt. 26:36-44)

Among other times in his earthly life, Jesus even prayed his final words and last breath of life on the cross (Luke 23; John 19; Matt. 27). He also taught on the importance of prayer (Matt. 21:22; Mark 11:24-26; Matt. 7:7-11; Luke 11:9-13; John 14:13-14; 15:7,16; 16:23-24; Matt. 5:44; Luke 6:27-28; Matt. 6:5-15), including the Lord's Prayer (Luke 11:2-4; Matt. 18:19-20). If you take all of the places that show Jesus praying, you will have a perfect outline for how best to pray (check out John 17 as the ultimate example of an upward, inward and outward prayer).

Why did Jesus pray, you might ask? First of all, Jesus prayed to be an example to his followers in highlighting the importance of a disciple's dependence upon the Father. He knew we would need this example as we struggle to follow God obediently and faithfully. Secondly, the Incarnation of Jesus consists of both his divine and human natures. Therefore, from his human nature, it was perfectly natural for a Jewish believer such as Christ to pray. Also, the nature of the Trinity encourages and affirms communication between its members. As God the Son, Jesus would freely pray to God the Father and in the Spirit. We too are encouraged to pray in the name of the Father, Son, and Holy Spirit. Or, more simply, in Jesus' name. Amen.

The following two entries are specifically devoted to Jesus' prayers. But, we must remember, with thanksgiving, that given Jesus' Trinitarian authority, the entirety of the Scriptures enlighten our understanding of his life of prayer. Hebrews 5:7 reminds us, "During the days of Jesus' life on earth, he offered up prayers and petitions with loud cries and tears to the one who could save him from death, and he was heard because of his reverent submission." May the perfect example of a praying Jesus inspire you to follow more fervently his loving example as you continue to learn how to pray.

Day 9

The Lord's Prayer

"Lord, teach us to pray" (Luke 11:1). What the disciples asked of Jesus could not have been more clear and straightforward. In the midst of his Sermon on the Mount (Matthew 5-7), Jesus instructs his disciples how best to pray. He sets this in contrast to how hypocrites show off in prayer, and instead offers wisdom in how to pray in hiddenness. The result of Jesus' teaching on prayer is that his followers have a road map to consider as they bow their heads and offer their lives back to the Savior. The context for such prayer is the intimacy Jesus offers to all who put their hope and confidence in his hands.

The Lord's Prayer has been a mainstay for Christians since the time of Christ. The elements contained in this epic prayer include the various ways one relates to the Father...in awe and reverence, acknowledging his love and lordship, his provisions and protection, his forgiveness and deliverance, his kingdom here and in heaven. With this guide to prayer, Christians are given great freedom to express our heart for God and our earnest praise, plea, petition, and prayer. Reflect on the Lord's Prayer. Consider how each phrase is richly loaded with meaning. Recite it slowly as if it's the first time you've encountered this way to pray. No babbling required.

Today...

Join Jesus and pray the Lord's Prayer (**Matthew 6: 5-15**)

And when you pray, do not be like the hypocrites, for they love to pray standing in the synagogues and on the street corners to be seen by others. Truly I tell you, they have received their reward in full. But when you pray, go into your room, close the door and pray to your Father, who is unseen. Then your Father, who sees what is done in secret, will reward you. And when you pray, do not keep on babbling like pagans, for they think they will be heard because of their many words. Do not be like them, for your Father knows what you need before you ask him.

This, then, is how you should pray:

Our Father in heaven,
hallowed be your name,
your kingdom come,
your will be done,
on earth as it is in heaven.
Give us today our daily bread.
And forgive us our debts,
as we also have forgiven our debtors.
And lead us not into temptation,
but deliver us from the evil one.
For if you forgive other people when they sin against you,
your heavenly Father will also forgive you.
But if you do not forgive others their sins, your Father will
not forgive your sins.

As you reflect on the Word, how is God inviting you to pray? What biblical words or phrases are you led to use in your own prayer?

_____

_____

_____

_____

_____

_____

_____

_____

_____

_____

_____

Behold the splendor of the Lord – Believe the promises of his love – Belong to those who unreservedly trust him – Become prayerful in all you are and do.

Day 10

Jesus' High Priestly Prayer

The heart of God has always been for unity and oneness among his people. This was true for the children of God in the Old Testament, as reflected in myriad stories from the Pentateuch to the Prophets, in the psalter, the proverbs, and in the historical books too. God has been urging his people to hold hands and stick together since our beginnings. He delights in our single-heartedness and one-mindedness. He is fully conscious of how the enemy of our souls can so easily wreak havoc upon the body of Christ, disturbing any form of loving togetherness.

Throughout the New Testament, unity is encouraged in and through the Spirit. Jesus' great high priestly prayer in John 17 is perhaps the pinnacle expression of God's distinct preference for unity among his own personhood, within the ranks of Jesus' disciples, and for generations of Christ-followers to follow. With unity on the mind of God and at the heart of the body of Christ, Jesus prays for his disciples to be reflections of the oneness of the God-head. The first third of the prayer (vs. 1-5) refers to the unity Jesus, the Father and the Spirit enjoy. This is followed by prayers for his immediate disciples (vs. 6-19), distinct from the portion we are praying today, which is for subsequent generations of believers (vs. 20-26). As you sit with this prayer, be mindful of God's specific invitation for you to be a builder of unity…so that the world may know and believe.

Today...

Join Jesus and pray for God's beloved disciples as witnesses of the love of God (John 17: 20-26)

My prayer is not for them alone. I pray also for those who will believe in me through their message, that all of them may be one, Father, just as you are in me and I am in you. May they also be in us so that the world may believe that you have sent me. I have given them the glory that you gave me, that they may be one as we are one— I in them and you in me—so that they may be brought to complete unity. Then the world will know that you sent me and have loved them even as you have loved me. Father, I want those you have given me to be with me where I am, and to see my glory, the glory you have given me because you loved me before the creation of the world. Righteous Father, though the world does not know you, I know you, and they know that you have sent me. I have made you known to them, and will continue to make you known in order that the love you have for me may be in them and that I myself may be in them.

As you reflect on the Word, how is God inviting you to pray? What biblical words or phrases are you led to use in your own prayer?

_____

_____

_____

_____

_____

_____

_____

_____

_____

_____

_____

_____

_____

Behold the splendor of the Lord – Believe the promises of his love – Belong to those who unreservedly trust him – Become prayerful in all you are and do.

The 7 Last Words of Jesus on the Cross

The Last Words of Jesus from the Cross were prayerful and profound. Consider the power of each of the following as you transition your biblical prayers from the lips of Jesus to those who heeded his voice and responded to his loving initiatives on their behalf.

1. **Jesus Speaks to the Father – His forgiveness for his executors and enemies**

   Jesus said, "Father, forgive them, for they do not know what they are doing." Luke 23:34

   In the midst of his excruciating suffering, Jesus focused on others rather than himself. Here we see the nature of his love—unconditional and divine.

2. **Jesus Speaks to the Criminal on the Cross – His forgiveness and salvation for the repentant**

   "I tell you the truth, today you will be with me in paradise." Luke 23:43

   One of the criminals who was crucified with Christ had recognized who Jesus was and expressed faith in him as Savior.

   Here we see God's grace poured out through faith, as Jesus assured the dying man of his forgiveness and eternal salvation.

3. Jesus Speaks to Mary and John – His care for his loved ones

When Jesus saw his mother there, and the disciple whom he loved standing nearby, he said to his mother, "Woman, here is your son," and to the disciple, "Here is your mother." John 19: 26-27

Jesus, looking down from the cross, was filled with the concerns of a son for the earthly needs of his mother. None of his brothers was there to care for her, so he gave this task to the Apostle John.

Here we clearly see Christ's humanity amidst his divinity.

4. Jesus Cries Out to the Father – His intimate honesty with the Father

And about the ninth hour Jesus cried out with a loud voice, saying, "Eli, Eli, lema sabachthani?" which means, "My God, My God, why have You forsaken Me?" Matt. 27:46; Mark 115:34

In the darkest hours of his suffering, Jesus cried out the opening words of Psalm 22. And although much has been suggested regarding the meaning of this phrase, it was quite apparent the agony Christ felt as he expressed separation from God. Here we see the Father turning away from the Son as Jesus bore the full weight of our sin.

5. **Jesus is Thirsty – His humanness being transformed to Divinity**
   Jesus knew that everything was now finished, and to fulfill the Scriptures he said, "I am thirsty." John 19:28

   Jesus refused the initial drink of vinegar, gall, and myrrh (Matthew 27:34 and Mark 15:23) offered to alleviate his suffering. But here, several hours later, we see Jesus fulfilling the messianic prophecy found in Psalm 69:21.

6. **It is Finished – His life on earth completed!**
   ... he said, "It is finished!" John 19:30

   Jesus knew he was suffering the crucifixion for a purpose. Earlier he had said in John 10:18 of his life, "No one takes it from me, but I lay it down of my own accord. I have authority to lay it down and authority to take it up again. This command I received from my Father." (NIV)

   These three words were packed with meaning, for what was finished here was not only Christ's earthly life, not only his suffering and dying, not only the payment for sin and the redemption of the world—but the very reason and purpose he came to earth was finished. His final act of obedience was complete. The Scriptures had been fulfilled.

7. Jesus' Last Words – His full submission, obedience, and glorification!

Jesus called out with a loud voice, "Father, into your hands I commit my spirit." When he had said this, he breathed his last. Luke 23:46

Here Jesus closes with the words of Psalm 31:5, speaking to the Father. We see his complete trust in the Father. Jesus entered death in the same way he lived each day of his life, offering up his life as the perfect sacrifice and placing himself in God's hands.

Day 11

Paul prays for the Churches in Philippi and Colossae

The Apostle Paul had great affection for the churches he established and the expansive work of the gospel of Jesus they shared in common. His prayers were always for their good unity, shared identity, and mission. "Grace and peace to you from God the Father and the Lord Jesus," combined with "the love of God and the fellowship of the Holy Spirit," are oft-repeated phrases that spring from the prayers of Paul. His greetings, benedictions, and exhortations in between were abundant in prayerful admonitions and instructions. Paul was a leader who knew what it was like to be dependent completely upon God and who exemplified this in his prayers.

In his prayers for the churches of Philippi and Colossae, we see some familiar themes: love, knowledge, insight, discernment, wisdom, fruitfulness, power, patience and endurance. Each of these topics is replete with meaning and application for the churches Paul founded and for the Church today. In considering these prayers we too are claiming the importance of these themes for our daily lives and shared ministries with others in the body of Christ. Our prayers are not for ourselves alone. They are for the good of the body of Christ and the mission we share as brothers and sisters on the journey together. May these prayers ignite your passion for serving in the Church, all the while increasing your fruitfulness in Christ.

Today...

Join Paul and pray for God's direction
(**Phil. 1:9-11**)

*And this is my prayer: that your love may abound more
and more in knowledge and depth of insight, so that you
may be able to discern what is best and may be pure and
blameless for the day of Christ, filled with the fruit of
righteousness that comes through Jesus Christ—to the glory
and praise of God.*

And pray with Paul for fruitfulness in our
passion and witness (**Col. 1: 9-14**)

*For this reason, since the day we heard about you, we have
not stopped praying for you. We continually ask God to fill
you with the knowledge of his will through all the wisdom
and understanding that the Spirit gives, so that you may
live a life worthy of the Lord and please him in every way:
bearing fruit in every good work, growing in the knowledge
of God, being strengthened with all power according to his
glorious might so that you may have great endurance and
patience, and giving joyful thanks to the Father, who has
qualified you to share in the inheritance of his holy people
in the kingdom of light. For he has rescued us from the
dominion of darkness and brought us into the kingdom of
the Son he loves, in whom we have redemption, the
forgiveness of sins.*

As you reflect on the Word, how is God inviting you to pray? What biblical words or phrases are you led to use in your own prayer?

_____

_____

_____

_____

_____

_____

_____

_____

_____

_____

_____

_____

Behold the splendor of the Lord – Believe the promises of his love – Belong to those who unreservedly trust him – Become prayerful in all you are and do.

Day 12

Paul prays for the Church in Ephesus

Paul was constantly urging his churches toward love and maturity in Christ. He was direct in his correctives and his encouragements. All that he offered to others was out of loving reverence for Christ. His posture among the churches he started and served was on what Jesus would expect of his followers. Paul held others to the highest of standards, knowing that the gospel was to be presented with fervor and joy in Christ…always. Paul's prayer for the church in Ephesus is for them to be filled with the indwelling presence and power of God, accompanied by the love of Christ which surpasses all human knowledge. All for the sake of being filled up with the fullness of God, who does immeasurably more than we could ever ask, dream or imagine.

On the heels of this prayer, he urges the Ephesians toward maturity and unity in Christ. Their maturity is to be evidenced in their humility, gentleness, patience, and forbearance. Their unity was to be unparalleled in any previous or forthcoming generation. Paul was continuously promoting unity of heart, mind, and mission, knowing that without oneness of heart and mind the church would wobble. His message was consistent: make every effort to keep the unity of the Spirit through the bond of peace. Imagine if our churches today were held to such considerable standards. Were it not for Christ, we could never attain such a goal.

Today…

Join Paul and pray for the unity and maturity of God's church (**Ephesians 3: 14-21**)

*For this reason I kneel before the Father, from whom every family in heaven and on earth derives its name. I pray that out of his glorious riches he may strengthen you with power through his Spirit in your inner being, so that Christ may dwell in your hearts through faith. And I pray that you, being rooted and established in love, may have power, together with all the Lord's holy people, to grasp how wide and long and high and deep is the love of Christ, and to know this love that surpasses knowledge—that you may be filled to the measure of all the fullness of God.
Now to him who is able to do immeasurably more than all we ask or imagine, according to his power that is at work within us, to him be glory in the church and in Christ Jesus throughout all generations, for ever and ever! Amen.*

As you reflect on the Word, how is God inviting you to pray? What biblical words or phrases are you led to use in your own prayer?

_____

_____

_____

_____

_____

_____

_____

_____

_____

_____

_____

Behold the splendor of the Lord – Believe the promises of his love – Belong to those who unreservedly trust him – Become prayerful in all you are and do.

Day 13

Peter, John and Believers

After the Holy Spirit arrives in the midst of the Early Church, Peter preaches to the community of the faithful ones. He proclaims what the prophet Joel once spoke about, "In the last days, God says, I will pour out my Spirit on all people...I will show wonders in the heavens above and signs on the earth below..." (Joel 2) and from David in Psalm 16, "...you have made known to me the paths of life; you will fill me with joy in your presence." Strengthened miraculously by the Spirit, the believers devoted themselves to teaching, fellowship, communion, and prayer. All of them shared their resources with one another, as their sincere hearts were filled with praise for God and fellowship with one another. It was a sweet time for all to enjoy.

But, as is often the case, immediately thereafter the persecution begins…first and foremost by the religious authorities. The priests, temple guards, and the Sadducees seized Peter and John, throwing them in prison for teaching the people and proclaiming in Jesus the resurrection of the dead. But that didn't stop Peter from being filled with the Spirit. His message of salvation in Christ alone astonished them all. A man who had been miraculously healed now sealed the leaders' need to free Peter and John, but with even more concern about how best to stop them in the future.

Upon their release (Acts 4: 23f), Peter and John return to their "own people" and report all that had occurred. Their immediate response: prayer. They raised their voices together in prayer to God, knowing that without the Lord's protection and provision their lives and ministries would be in jeopardy.

Today…

Join Peter, John, and the Early Church and pray for healing and strength for the journey of faith in the midst of persecution (**Acts 4: 23-31**)

"Sovereign Lord," they said, "you made the heavens and the earth and the sea, and everything in them. You spoke by the Holy Spirit through the mouth of your servant, our father David:

Why do the nations rage
and the peoples plot in vain?
The kings of the earth rise up
and the rulers band together
against the Lord
and against his anointed one.

Indeed Herod and Pontius Pilate met together with the Gentiles and the people of Israel in this city to conspire against your holy servant Jesus, whom you anointed. They did what your power and will had decided beforehand should happen. Now, Lord, consider their threats and enable your servants to speak your word with great boldness. Stretch out your hand to heal and perform signs and wonders through the name of your holy servant Jesus."

After they prayed, the place where they were meeting was shaken. And they were all filled with the Holy Spirit and spoke the word of God boldly.

As you reflect on the Word, how is God inviting you to pray? What biblical words or phrases are you led to use in your own prayer?

_____

_____

_____

_____

_____

_____

_____

_____

_____

_____

_____

_____

Behold the splendor of the Lord – Believe the promises of his love – Belong to those who unreservedly trust him – Become prayerful in all you are and do.

Day 14

Stephen

The Church admires the wisdom the Spirit of God gave to Stephen, a man full of God's grace and power. He stood up against the leaders of his day and proclaimed the truth about Jesus. These leaders, irritated by his bold proclamation of the gospel, could hardly tolerate Stephen. But, they simply could not stand up against the wisdom the Spirit gave him as he spoke. When the Sanhedrin summoned Stephen, they looked intently at Stephen "and they saw that his face was like the face of an angel" (Acts 6:10, 15). His speech to the Sanhedrin (Acts 7) was stunning and worth rereading to bolster one's faith in the glory and truth of God. Stephen started with the story of Moses up to the time of David, inserting the prophet Isaiah's words to drive home his point: the people have resisted the Holy Spirit and for generations they have been a stiff-necked people.

When the Sanhedrin heard all that Stephen said, they were furious. They gnashed their teeth at him. But Stephen kept his eyes on the Lord…and this enraged them all the more. They rushed at him and dragged him out of the city. They began to stone him. Stephen died a martyr's death on that day. Persecution continued to mount against the Church. It became harder and all the more challenging to follow Jesus from that time on. Believers were scattered throughout Judea and Samaria.

Today…

Join Stephen in his simple prayers of faithful perseverance and forgiving grace amidst those who resisted his proclamation of the gospel, even as you consider those who are against what you stand for today as a follower of Jesus
(**Acts 7: 54-60**)

When the members of the Sanhedrin heard this, they were furious and gnashed their teeth at him. But Stephen, full of the Holy Spirit, looked up to heaven and saw the glory of God, and Jesus standing at the right hand of God. "Look," he said, "I see heaven open and the Son of Man standing at the right hand of God." (vs. 56)

At this they covered their ears and, yelling at the top of their voices, they all rushed at him, dragged him out of the city and began to stone him. Meanwhile, the witnesses laid their coats at the feet of a young man named Saul.

While they were stoning him, Stephen prayed, "Lord Jesus, receive my spirit." (vs. 59)

Then Stephen fell on his knees and cried out, "Lord, do not hold this sin against them." (vs. 60)

When he had said this, he fell asleep.

As you reflect on the Word, how is God inviting you to pray? What biblical words or phrases are you led to use in your own prayer?

_____

_____

_____

_____

_____

_____

_____

_____

_____

_____

_____

_____

Behold the splendor of the Lord – Believe the promises of his love – Belong to those who unreservedly trust him – Become prayerful in all you are and do.

Day 15

Revelation of John Part One

G od made known the revelation from Jesus Christ by sending an angel to his servant John, who testified to everything he saw. The Word of God and the testimony of Jesus Christ blessed John and all who heard with their hearts the proclamation of the glory of God. The major themes contained within Revelation all center on the proclamation of Jesus, his power, majesty, dominion, and peace. Grace, mercy, justice, sovereignty, and wisdom envelop his eternal plan. Let's recount together some of the great prayers of praise to Almighty God recorded for us in the book of Revelation.

Today…

Join John the Apostle in praise to the Lord God Almighty. Let these words refresh and renew you, washing over your soul with grace and tenderness, joy and delight.
(Revelation 4: 8, 11; 5: 9, 10, 12, 13)

"Holy, holy, holy is the Lord God Almighty, who was, and is, and is to come." (4:8)

"You are worthy, our Lord and God, to receive glory and honor and power, for you created all things, and by your will they were created and have their being." (4:11)

"You are worthy to take the scroll and to open its seals, because you were slain, and with your blood you purchased for God persons from every tribe and language and people and nation. You have made them to be a kingdom and priests to serve our God, and they will reign on the earth." (5: 9,10)

"Worthy is the Lamb, who was slain, to receive power and wealth and wisdom and strength and honor and glory and praise!" (5:11)

"Then I heard every creature in heaven and on earth and under the earth and on the sea, and all that is in them, saying: 'To him who sits on the throne and to the Lamb be praise and honor and glory and power, for ever and ever!" (5:12,13)

"Amen!"

As you reflect on the Word, how is God inviting you to pray? What biblical words or phrases are you led to use in your own prayer?

_____

_____

_____

_____

_____

_____

_____

_____

_____

_____

_____

_____

_____

Behold the splendor of the Lord – Believe the promises of his love – Belong to those who unreservedly trust him – Become prayerful in all you are and do.

Day 16

Revelation of John – Part Two

God's angel continues to disclose the Revelation to John. Notice the marvelous prayers offered within the text drawn directly from the prophets and the psalms. These are wonderfully refreshing to believers of all generations. They help us construct our own prayer templates for praising, honoring and glorifying God. With the final book of the Bible so focused on praise, one can't help but notice the many powerful ways we are to offer our praise to God. Imagine how different your life would be if it were highlighted by praise and joy, thanksgiving and blessing to Almighty God. Ponder these powerful prayers from the book of Revelation. Be open to how the manifold blessings of God have been revealed to you in your daily life and relationships. May all that you are and all that you hold dear reflect your praise to the Lord. He has given you all that life has to offer this side of heaven and for all eternity. Praise the Lord!

Today...

Join John the Apostle as he records for us the prayerful words of Scripture and then sing these songs of praise in your heart back to the Lord in prayer. (**Rev. 15, 19**)

"Great and marvelous are your deeds, Lord God Almighty. Just and true are your ways, King of the nations. Who will not fear you, Lord, and bring glory to your name? For you alone are holy. All nations will come and worship before you, for your righteous acts have been revealed."
(Rev. 15: 3,4)

"Hallelujah! Salvation and glory and power belong to our God, for true and just are his judgments. He has condemned the great prostitute who corrupted the earth by her adulteries. He has avenged on her the blood of his servants. And again they shouted: Hallelujah! Amen, Hallelujah! For our Lord God Almighty reigns. Let us rejoice and be glad and give him glory! For the wedding of the Lamb has come, and his bride has made herself ready. Fine linen, bright and clean, was given her to wear. (Fine linen stands for the righteous acts of God's holy people." (Rev. 19: 1-8)

As you reflect on the Word, how is God inviting you to pray? What biblical words or phrases are you led to use in your own prayer?

_____

_____

_____

_____

_____

_____

_____

_____

_____

_____

_____

_____

_____

_____

Behold the splendor of the Lord – Believe the promises of his love – Belong to those who unreservedly trust him – Become prayerful in all you are and do.

Praying the Psalms

Throughout this devotional we have joined some of our favorite biblical characters in the prayers they once prayed. For us God has preserved these prayers in the Scriptures. Ponder the variety of prayers from the Great Prayer Book, the Psalms. Be enveloped by each word. God wrote each word directly to and for you, His gift for your soul today. Praying the Scriptures in this way will bring health and vitality to your heart and soul, and great liberty to your life of prayer.

Come home, o my soul, through the ever-flourishing prayer book, the Psalms.

Day 17

Psalm 1, 19 and 119 – Blessed is the one who delights in the law of the Lord

Psalm 1 opens to a theme portrayed dramatically and variably throughout the Psalter: the human heart in dire need of God. The psalmist reminds us that without a pure delight in the law of the Lord, meditating on it day and night, we will be easily swayed in the direction of the wicked, the sinners, and the company of mockers. Delight yourself in the law of God. Plant yourself next to the Word. In so doing you will experience the richness of a spiritually prosperous life. Psalms 19 and 119 are additional readings for reflection that reinforce the centrality of the Word of God in our personal spiritual formation.

Today...

Join the psalmist in pledging your heart to be like a tree planted firmly by a stream of living water, delighting in the law of the Lord (**Psalm 1**)

Blessed is the one
who does not walk in step with the wicked
or stand in the way that sinners take
or sit in the company of mockers,
but whose delight is in the law of the LORD,
and who meditates on his law day and night.
That person is like a tree planted by streams of water,
which yields its fruit in season
and whose leaf does not wither—
whatever they do prospers.
Not so the wicked!
They are like chaff
that the wind blows away.
Therefore the wicked will not stand in the judgment,
nor sinners in the assembly of the righteous.
For the LORD *watches over the way of the righteous,*
but the way of the wicked leads to destruction.

As you reflect on the Word, how is God inviting you to pray? What biblical words or phrases are you led to use in your own prayer?

_____

_____

_____

_____

_____

_____

_____

_____

_____

_____

_____

_____

_____

Behold the splendor of the Lord – Believe the promises of his love – Belong to those who unreservedly trust him – Become prayerful in all you are and do.

Day 18

Psalm 8 – Who am I that you are mindful of me?

Psalm 8 declares the majesty of the Lord. He set his glory in the heavens, the work of his fingers, placing the moon and the stars according to his will. So in contrast who are we, also created beings, but much lower in stature than the angels who are crowned with glory and honor? The psalm reminds us: God is very mindful of us human beings. Just like the moon and stars have perfect placement, so we too have a divine destiny…to rule over the works of God's hands. Be reminded that the God who created us in the first place is the One who knows all the intricacies of our lives. This psalm is a comfort to all who follow God and choose the with-God life.

Today...

As you sit with this psalm and reflect on the mindfulness of God toward you, his beloved child, let your heart swell with thanksgiving and praise. (**Psalm 8**)

Lord, our Lord,
how majestic is your name in all the earth!
You have set your glory in the heavens.
Through the praise of children and infants
you have established a stronghold against your enemies,
to silence the foe and the avenger.
When I consider your heavens,
the work of your fingers,
the moon and the stars,
which you have set in place,
what is mankind that you are mindful of them,
human beings that you care for them?
You have made them a little lower than the angels
and crowned them with glory and honor.
You made them rulers over the works of your hands;
you put everything under their feet:
all flocks and herds, and the animals of the wild,
the birds in the sky,
and the fish in the sea,
all that swim the paths of the seas.
Lord, our Lord, how majestic
is your name in all the earth!

As you reflect on the Word, how is God inviting you to pray? What biblical words or phrases are you led to use in your own prayer?

_____

_____

_____

_____

_____

_____

_____

_____

_____

_____

_____

_____

_____

Behold the splendor of the Lord – Believe the promises of his love – Belong to those who unreservedly trust him – Become prayerful in all you are and do.

Day 19

Psalm 16 – You make known to me the path of life

Deemed the "golden psalm" or "David's jewel," Psalm 16 is a Messianic psalm pointing to the coming of Christ and his ministry of deliverance and direction. I chose this psalm as the thematic psalm for my book, *Crafting a Rule of Life*, out of recognition that the Lord is the One in whom we take refuge, the One who is our delight, the One who is our daily portion and cup, the One who counsels and instructs us, and the One who holds us eternally secure. The Lord Jesus makes the way for us to walk along our own "path of life" both now and forevermore. Jesus is the One to whom we listen attentively as we journey through this life and into the next. Therefore, our hearts rejoice in his presence and our joy will be found in the Lord alone, both now and forevermore.

Today...

As you give thanks to the Lord for the provision
of his Son Jesus as your refuge and redeemer,
offer your true self into the fullness of his will
as you walk the path of life created just for
you. (**Psalm 16**)

Keep me safe, my God,
for in you I take refuge.
I say to the LORD, "You are my Lord;
apart from you I have no good thing."
I say of the holy people who are in the land,
"They are the noble ones in whom is all my delight."
Those who run after other gods will suffer more and more.
I will not pour out libations of blood to such gods
or take up their names on my lips.
LORD, you alone are my portion and my cup;
you make my lot secure.
The boundary lines have fallen for me in pleasant places;
surely I have a delightful inheritance.
I will praise the LORD, who counsels me;
even at night my heart instructs me.
I keep my eyes always on the LORD.
With him at my right hand, I will not be shaken.
Therefore my heart is glad and my tongue rejoices;
my body also will rest secure,
because you will not abandon me to the realm of the dead,

nor will you let your faithful one see decay.
You make known to me the path of life;
you will fill me with joy in your presence,
with eternal pleasures at your right hand.

As you reflect on the Word, how is God inviting you to pray? What biblical words or phrases are you led to use in your own prayer?

_____

_____

_____

_____

_____

_____

_____

_____

_____

_____

_____

Behold the splendor of the Lord – Believe the promises of his love – Belong to those who unreservedly trust him – Become prayerful in all you are and do.

Day 20

Psalm 23 – You, Lord, are my Shepherd

For thousands of years children and adults have memorized Psalm 23, by far the most popular of all the psalms. Treasured at times of loss and grief, this psalm has provided comfort and hope for generations of believers worldwide. At its core, Psalm 23 is the Shepherd's psalm, written by David during his old age, reminiscent of his years as a shepherd boy and analogous to the Good Shepherd of his soul, the Lord himself. When Jesus comes into this world, he identifies himself as the Good Shepherd who knows all his sheep by name (John 10). He stands in contrast to the wolves of this age who taunt, trick and tire out the sheep within the sheepfold. Listen to the Good Shepherd in this psalm. Be comforted and refreshed by the whispering presence of his loving concern for you... for you to be without want, to be lovingly held down in green pastures, to be led by quiet waters, to be restored in your soul, to be led down paths of righteousness, and to be present with him forevermore.

Today…

As the Good Shepherd comforts you with his provision and protection, pledge your heart to His and be drawn back into the safety of the sheepfold forevermore (**Psalm 23**).

The LORD is my shepherd, I lack nothing.
He makes me lie down in green pastures,
he leads me beside quiet waters, he refreshes my soul.
He guides me along the right paths
for his name's sake.
Even though I walk
through the darkest valley,
I will fear no evil,
for you are with me;
your rod and your staff,
they comfort me.
You prepare a table before me
in the presence of my enemies.
You anoint my head with oil;
my cup overflows.
Surely your goodness and love will follow me
all the days of my life,
and I will dwell in the house of the LORD
forever.

As you reflect on the Word, how is God inviting you to pray? What biblical words or phrases are you led to use in your own prayer?

_____

_____

_____

_____

_____

_____

_____

_____

_____

_____

_____

_____

Behold the splendor of the Lord – Believe the promises of his love – Belong to those who unreservedly trust him – Become prayerful in all you are and do.

Day 21

Psalm 25 – Show me, Teach me, Guide me

Praying the psalms helps us bring before God our genuine heart cries evoked by real life. In this psalm we see many such longings: to put our trust in the Living God, who doesn't put us to shame and doesn't allow our human, cultural or demonic enemies to rot our soul with their influence. Out of such protection, this psalm prays for direction: Lord, show me, teach me, and guide me in your truth and then toward your pathway of hope, mercy and love for me. This psalm is a prayerful remembrance of all that God has done in the past to heal, redeem, forgive, provide and protect. The latter part of the psalm is a plea for grace and relief from the pangs of this world and for God to be the one to guard, rescue and protect our integrity. Praying this psalm allows the believer to put everything out on the table with earnestness and authenticity.

Today…

Join the psalmist with your own intercession for a trusting, protective, empowering life in, through and with God, the lover of your hope-filled soul. (**Psalm 25**)

In you, Lord my God, I put my trust
I trust in you;
do not let me be put to shame,
nor let my enemies triumph over me.
No one who hopes in you
will ever be put to shame,
but shame will come on those
who are treacherous without cause.
Show me your ways, Lord,
teach me your paths.
Guide me in your truth and teach me,
for you are God my Savior,
and my hope is in you all day long.
Remember, Lord, your great mercy and love,
for they are from of old.
Do not remember the sins of my youth
and my rebellious ways;
according to your love remember me,
for you, Lord, are good.
Good and upright is the Lord;
therefore he instructs sinners in his ways.
He guides the humble in what is right

and teaches them his way.
All the ways of the Lord are loving and faithful
toward those who keep the demands of his covenant.
For the sake of your name, Lord,
forgive my iniquity, though it is great.
Who, then, are those who fear the Lord?
He will instruct them in the ways they should choose.
They will spend their days in prosperity,
and their descendants will inherit the land.
The Lord confides in those who fear him;
he makes his covenant known to them.
My eyes are ever on the Lord,
for only he will release my feet from the snare.
Turn to me and be gracious to me,
for I am lonely and afflicted.
Relieve the troubles of my heart
and free me from my anguish.
Look on my affliction and my distress
and take away all my sins.
See how numerous are my enemies
and how fiercely they hate me!
Guard my life and rescue me;
do not let me be put to shame,
for I take refuge in you.
May integrity and uprightness protect me,
because my hope, Lord, is in you.
Deliver Israel, O God,
from all their troubles!

As you reflect on the Word, how is God inviting you to pray? What biblical words or phrases are you led to use in your own prayer?

_____

_____

_____

_____

_____

_____

_____

_____

_____

_____

_____

_____

Behold the splendor of the Lord – Believe the promises of his love – Belong to those who unreservedly trust him – Become prayerful in all you are and do.

Day 22

Psalm 42 – My soul pants for you

Panting and thirsting are words that describe deep calling out deeper still in the prayers of the saints. This psalm is often combined with the subsequent psalm (43) as if they were one. Notice the similarities, especially in the desire to be rescued in the midst of feeling downcast. What's so life giving about this psalm is the language of raw and honest longing for God. Panting, tears, pouring out, shouts of joy and praise, downcast, disturbed, forgotten, mourning, suffering, agony, all combined as an orchestral cacophony of internal clamoring for hope in the Lord. The richness of the text comes alive in our hearing and is strengthened all the more in our use of these expressions in our own prayers. We all suffer similarly. We experience tears in the watches of the night. We wonder if God remembers us. We thirst for the same thing: the presence, power and peace of the Living God.

Today...

As you give yourself permission to fully enter
this prayerful psalm of longing, let your heart
swell up with thanksgiving that God accepts you
just as you are and can handle all of your ranting
and every single panting for more and more of
his gifts of grace, mercy and love (**Psalm 42**).

As the deer pants for streams of water,
so my soul pants for you, my God.
My soul thirsts for God, for the living God.
When can I go and meet with God?
My tears have been my food
day and night,
while people say to me all day long,
"Where is your God?"
These things I remember
as I pour out my soul:
how I used to go to the house of God
under the protection of the Mighty One
with shouts of joy and praise
among the festive throng.
Why, my soul, are you downcast?
Why so disturbed within me?
Put your hope in God,
for I will yet praise him,
my Savior and my God.
My soul is downcast within me;

therefore I will remember you
from the land of the Jordan,
the heights of Hermon—from Mount Mizar.
Deep calls to deep
in the roar of your waterfalls;
all your waves and breakers
have swept over me.
By day the Lord directs his love,
at night his song is with me—
a prayer to the God of my life.
I say to God my Rock,
"Why have you forgotten me?
Why must I go about mourning,
oppressed by the enemy?"
My bones suffer mortal agony
as my foes taunt me,
saying to me all day long,
"Where is your God?"
Why, my soul, are you downcast?
Why so disturbed within me?
Put your hope in God,
for I will yet praise him,
my Savior and my God.

As you reflect on the Word, how is God inviting you to pray? What biblical words or phrases are you led to use in your own prayer?

_____

_____

_____

_____

_____

_____

_____

_____

_____

_____

_____

_____

_____

Behold the splendor of the Lord – Believe the promises of his love – Belong to those who unreservedly trust him – Become prayerful in all you are and do.

Day 23

Psalm 46 – Be still and know God

Psalm 46 reminds us to attend to the ways God has been our refuge and our strength, an ever-present help in times of trouble. Therefore, we shall not fear…no matter what circumstances befall us, consume us, or seek to overwhelm us. God's desire has been and always will be to protect and provide for his beloved children. All we need to do is stop long enough to remember the many ways he has done so over the generations and throughout our own lives. At the end of verses 3, 7 and 11 the psalmist inserts the word "Selah" (not shown here). For many scholars, "Selah" means "pause." How fitting for us to do so on a regular basis. At the pinnacle of this psalm, there is the dramatic call: "Be still and know that I am God." When we quiet the sounds and diminish the activities, slow down the rhythms and cease the tireless pursuits of this world, and simply still ourselves in the midst of this crazed world…then and only then will we know the ways of God. The deepest forms of prayer always include stillness, which leads to greater attentiveness.

Today...

Hop off the treadmill of your fast-paced drivenness to succeed and simply pursue stillness before God. Seek to know him more deeply. Recognize once more that he is indeed your refuge and strength, an ever-present help in times of trouble, turmoil and tempest. Be... still...and...know...(**Psalm 46**)

God is our refuge and strength,
an ever-present help in trouble.
Therefore we will not fear, though the earth give way
and the mountains fall into the heart of the sea,
though its waters roar and foam
and the mountains quake with their surging.
There is a river whose streams make glad the city of God,
the holy place where the Most High dwells.
God is within her, she will not fall;
God will help her at break of day.
Nations are in uproar, kingdoms fall;
he lifts his voice, the earth melts.
The Lord Almighty is with us;
the God of Jacob is our fortress.
Come and see what the Lord has done,
the desolations he has brought on the earth.
He makes wars cease
to the ends of the earth.
He breaks the bow and shatters the spear;

he burns the shields with fire.
He says, "Be still, and know that I am God;
I will be exalted among the nations,
I will be exalted in the earth."
The Lord Almighty is with us;
the God of Jacob is our fortress.

As you reflect on the Word, how is God inviting you to pray? What biblical words or phrases are you led to use in your own prayer?

_____

_____

_____

_____

_____

_____

_____

_____

_____

_____

_____

_____

Behold the splendor of the Lord – Believe the promises of his love – Belong to those who unreservedly trust him – Become prayerful in all you are and do.

Day 24

Psalm 55 – A Shelter from the Tempest and Storm

Casting all of our cares upon the Lord is a daily invitation to trust God with every fiber of our being. Only then will we know the full meaning of the word "sustain." Thankfully, that's exactly what God delights to do...sustain and protect us as we put our trust and hope in his hands, despite the circumstances of our lives. Psalm 55 is filled with internal and external rancor. The psalmist (David) is aware of what plagues him. His thoughts are troubling. He's in distress. His heart is in anguish, with fear and trembling lurking around the corner. He's also fully conscious of his external enemies and those who are opposed to him, as expressed in their anger, suffering, threats, confusion, violence, strife, malice, insult, and abuse. What's so enduring about this psalm is that it's all laid out before us and deemed acceptable to recount in prayer. How are we to pray for enemies both within and without? The psalmist, by example, encourages us to name them, acknowledge their presence, and ask God to sustain us in their midst. "Oh, that I had the wings of a dove! I would fly away and be at rest, I would flee far away and stay in the desert, I would hurry to my place of shelter, far from the tempest and storm." God indeed is our shelter amidst every form of suffering that comes our way. Will you invite the Lord to sustain you in your darkness and offer you his hand to protect you from your internal and external enemies?

Today…

Join the psalmist in offering your own litany of distress, inviting God to protect and sustain you, deepening your trust in his sheltering love (**Psalm 55**).

Listen to my prayer, O God,
do not ignore my plea;
hear me and answer me.
My thoughts trouble me and I am distraught
because of what my enemy is saying,
because of the threats of the wicked;
for they bring down suffering on me
and assail me in their anger.
My heart is in anguish within me;
the terrors of death have fallen on me.
Fear and trembling have beset me;
horror has overwhelmed me.
I said, "Oh, that I had the wings of a dove!
I would fly away and be at rest.
I would flee far away
and stay in the desert;
I would hurry to my place of shelter,
far from the tempest and storm."
Lord, confuse the wicked, confound their words,
for I see violence and strife in the city.
Day and night they prowl about on its walls;
malice and abuse are within it.

Destructive forces are at work in the city;
threats and lies never leave its streets.
If an enemy were insulting me,
I could endure it;
if a foe were rising against me,
I could hide.
But it is you, a man like myself,
my companion, my close friend,
with whom I once enjoyed sweet fellowship
at the house of God,
as we walked about
among the worshipers.
Let death take my enemies by surprise;
let them go down alive to the realm of the dead,
for evil finds lodging among them.
As for me, I call to God,
and the LORD SAVES ME.
Evening, morning and noon
I cry out in distress,
and he hears my voice.
He rescues me unharmed
from the battle waged against me,
even though many oppose me.
God, who is enthroned from of old,
who does not change—
he will hear them and humble them,
because they have no fear of God.
My companion attacks his friends;
he violates his covenant.

His talk is smooth as butter,
yet war is in his heart;
his words are more soothing than oil,
yet they are drawn swords.
Cast your cares on the LORD
and he will sustain you;
he will never let
the righteous be shaken.
But you, God, will bring down the wicked
into the pit of decay;
the bloodthirsty and deceitful
will not live out half their days.
But as for me, I trust in you.

As you reflect on the Word, how is God inviting you to pray? What biblical words or phrases are you led to use in your own prayer?

_____

_____

_____

_____

_____

_____

_____

_____

_____

_____

_____

_____

_____

Behold the splendor of the Lord – Believe the promises of his love – Belong to those who unreservedly trust him – Become prayerful in all you are and do.

Day 25

Psalm 62 – My soul finds rest in God alone

Psalm 62 begins with seven words that will change your life: "Truly my soul finds rest in God." Memorize them. Breathe them as a prayer throughout your day. When work or school, family or friends, accomplishments or success, or even sadness or shame, seek to reign over your heart and pull you away from true, everlasting peace…remember that only God can offer deep and abiding rest. It's only in God, our rock and our salvation, where we will discover our eternal hope and our reward. We so often look over our shoulder in the direction of others' plenty. Their delight becomes our comparative want. We lean away from the gospel truth and find ourselves on the tottering fence of jealous contempt. Instead, when we keep our eyes on the living God, trusting in him at all times, and pouring out our hearts to the One who matters most, we will truly find rest for our soul.

Today…

Join the psalmist in declaring your wholehearted trust in God. Desire nothing less than the unfailing love only he can provide. With honest confession, give voice to your temptation to trust in the things of this world more than the one thing that matters most: finding our truest rest in God alone (**Psalm 62**).

Truly my soul finds rest in God;
my salvation comes from him.
Truly he is my rock and my salvation;
he is my fortress, I will never be shaken.
How long will you assault me?
Would all of you throw me down—
this leaning wall, this tottering fence?
Surely they intend to topple me
from my lofty place;
they take delight in lies.
With their mouths they bless,
but in their hearts they curse.
Yes, my soul, find rest in God;
my hope comes from him.
Truly he is my rock and my salvation;
he is my fortress, I will not be shaken.
My salvation and my honor depend on God;
he is my mighty rock, my refuge.
Trust in him at all times, you people;

pour out your hearts to him,
for God is our refuge.
Surely the lowborn are but a breath,
the highborn are but a lie.
If weighed on a balance, they are nothing;
together they are only a breath.
Do not trust in extortion
or put vain hope in stolen goods;
though your riches increase,
do not set your heart on them.
One thing God has spoken,
two things I have heard:
Power belongs to you, God,
and with you, Lord, is unfailing love;
and, You reward everyone
according to what they have done.

As you reflect on the Word, how is God inviting you to pray? What biblical words or phrases are you led to use in your own prayer?

_____

_____

_____

_____

_____

_____

_____

_____

_____

_____

_____

_____

Behold the splendor of the Lord – Believe the promises of his love – Belong to those who unreservedly trust him – Become prayerful in all you are and do.

Day 26

Psalm 63 – On my bed I remember you

What is it you desire most in this life? Is it to behold the power and glory of God? Each time you see beauty in the sanctuaries of this earth, cry out in your heart with delight. Praise the Lord, for his love is better than life. And that love has been displayed before us in the radiant colors of his creation, in the enjoyment of fellowship with his people, in the splendor of worship in our communities of faith, and in the witness we offer to the world in Jesus' name. Raise your arms sing with joy as you experience firsthand the majesty and glory of God. God wants to open our eyes, ears, and hearts so that we readily receive all that God delights to offer those whom he loves with an infinite, matchless love.

Today…

Voice what your soul hungers for. Let your whole being give witness to the praise and glory of God. Because the Lord is, was and will be your help, remember him in the light of day and through the watches of the night. Give thanks to the Lord, and as you glorify him with your lips and your life, trust him prayerfully with your entire being (**Psalm 63**).

You, God, are my God,
earnestly I seek you;
I thirst for you,
my whole being longs for you,
in a dry and parched land
where there is no water.
I have seen you in the sanctuary
and beheld your power and your glory.
Because your love is better than life,
my lips will glorify you.
I will praise you as long as I live,
and in your name I will lift up my hands.
I will be fully satisfied as with the richest of foods;
with singing lips my mouth will praise you.
On my bed I remember you;
I think of you through the watches of the night.
Because you are my help,
I sing in the shadow of your wings.

I cling to you;
your right hand upholds me.
Those who want to kill me will be destroyed;
they will go down to the depths of the earth.
They will be given over to the sword
and become food for jackals.
But the king will rejoice in God;
all who swear by God will glory in him,
while the mouths of liars will be silenced.

As you reflect on the Word, how is God inviting you to pray? What biblical words or phrases are you led to use in your own prayer?

_____

_____

_____

_____

_____

_____

_____

_____

_____

_____

_____

_____

Behold the splendor of the Lord – Believe the promises of his love – Belong to those who unreservedly trust him – Become prayerful in all you are and do.

Day 27

Psalm 84 – Better is one day in your house

Where does your heart dwell most frequently in a typical day? Are you focused on remaining in a posture that leans toward God continually, day and night? Or, do you find yourself wandering away from the presence of God, lured into places where you don't belong? It's easy to forget the best location for the sake of our heart and soul. It's easy to let the influence of the world penetrate the very spaces where God alone seeks to reside. When we become soul lazy, we allow attitudes and their accompanying words fester and emerge…or, worse yet, we let them become actions that do not befit the follower of Christ. In Psalm 84, we are reminded that the best place for our soul is the dwelling place of God, the very court of the Lord, a home, a nest, a place near the altar, the safe and anointed house of God. It's the opposite of the tent of the wicked. It's the most inviting place of loveliness for our soul to yearn for this side of heaven.

Today...

Join the psalmist in a pilgrimage of the heart and soul directly into the presence of the Lord. Find your rest, your intentionality, your soul's home near the altar, so that the Lord Almighty, your King and your God may bless you for praising him and grant you the strength you need for the day's journey. Make this your prayer too.
(Psalm 84)

How lovely is your dwelling place,
Lord Almighty!
My soul yearns, even faints,
for the courts of the Lord;
my heart and my flesh cry out
for the living God.
Even the sparrow has found a home,
and the swallow a nest for herself,
where she may have her young—
a place near your altar,
Lord Almighty, my King and my God.
Blessed are those who dwell in your house;
they are ever praising you.
Blessed are those whose strength is in you,
whose hearts are set on pilgrimage.
As they pass through the Valley of Baka,
they make it a place of springs;
the autumn rains also cover it with pools.

They go from strength to strength,
till each appears before God in Zion.
Hear my prayer, Lord God Almighty;
listen to me, God of Jacob.
Look on our shield, O God;
look with favor on your anointed one.
Better is one day in your courts
than a thousand elsewhere;
I would rather be a doorkeeper in the house of my God
than dwell in the tents of the wicked.
For the Lord God is a sun and shield;
the Lord bestows favor and honor;
no good thing does he withhold
from those whose walk is blameless.
Lord Almighty,
blessed is the one who trusts in you.

As you reflect on the Word, how is God inviting you to pray? What biblical words or phrases are you led to use in your own prayer?

_____

_____

_____

_____

_____

_____

_____

_____

_____

_____

_____

_____

Behold the splendor of the Lord – Believe the promises of his love – Belong to those who unreservedly trust him – Become prayerful in all you are and do.

Day 28

Psalm 103 – Forget not all his benefits

What is it about your relationship with the Lord that evokes your praise? If you were to sit and offer prayers of praise to God, what would be on your heart and lips? In this great psalm, David sings his praise to the Triune God, celebrating the many gifts God has provided with abundant generosity. His soul is filled to overflowing with praise from his inmost being. He calls out these many gifts as benefits. His offering of praise is so the proceeds for his soul are never forgotten. He cites them as forgiveness, healing, redemption, love, compassion, satisfaction, righteousness, justice, graciousness, and love. Can you embrace these words as embodiments of your own offerings of praise and thanksgiving? If so, then let praise flow freely from the depth of your being and sing your prayer of joy to the Lord for offering these plentiful gifts to you each and every day of your life.

Today…

May your prayer be one of praise! Follow the outline offered by the psalmist and shout aloud your own offering of gratitude to the Lord for the many benefits he showers upon all who call upon his name with reverence, beauty and joyful delight. Flourish today in God's beneficial love and compassionate grace (**Psalm 103**).

Praise the Lord, my soul;
all my inmost being, praise his holy name.
Praise the Lord, my soul,
and forget not all his benefits—
who forgives all your sins
and heals all your diseases,
who redeems your life from the pit
and crowns you with love and compassion,
who satisfies your desires with good things
so that your youth is renewed like the eagle's.
The Lord works righteousness
and justice for all the oppressed.
He made known his ways to Moses,
his deeds to the people of Israel:
The Lord is compassionate and gracious,
slow to anger, abounding in love.
He will not always accuse,
nor will he harbor his anger forever;
he does not treat us as our sins deserve

or repay us according to our iniquities.
For as high as the heavens are above the earth,
so great is his love for those who fear him;
as far as the east is from the west,
so far has he removed our transgressions from us.
As a father has compassion on his children,
so the Lord has compassion on those who fear him;
for he knows how we are formed,
he remembers that we are dust.
The life of mortals is like grass,
they flourish like a flower of the field;
the wind blows over it and it is gone,
and its place remembers it no more.
But from everlasting to everlasting
the Lord's love is with those who fear him,
and his righteousness with their children's children—
with those who keep his covenant
and remember to obey his precepts.
The Lord has established his throne in heaven,
and his kingdom rules over all.
Praise the Lord, you his angels,
you mighty ones who do his bidding,
who obey his word.
Praise the Lord, all his heavenly hosts,
you his servants who do his will.
Praise the Lord, all his works
everywhere in his dominion.
Praise the Lord, my soul.

As you reflect on the Word, how is God inviting you to pray? What biblical words or phrases are you led to use in your own prayer?

_____

_____

_____

_____

_____

_____

_____

_____

_____

_____

_____

_____

_____

Behold the splendor of the Lord – Believe the promises of his love – Belong to those who unreservedly trust him – Become prayerful in all you are and do.

Day 29

Psalm 121 – I lift up my eyes to the hills

In times of need, both great and small, where do you look for help? Do you search elsewhere for your answers and seek the wisdom and aid of human sources, or do you look to God alone? In prayer, we are learning to focus our gaze upward to the Lord, the Maker of heaven and earth, and the intimate Author of our lives. In this psalm of ascent – one of the 15 in the psalter (120-134) – we recall with the people of Israel the songs they would recite together as they ascended the road to Jerusalem during special holy days. Here we focus on the Lord's protection over his beloved family. Imagine hearing the elders recite with boldness this amazing declaration, inviting their fellow pilgrims to sing along with gusto, "My help comes from the Lord." This reminds us that no matter what the Lord gives us to steward He will help us.Our feet will not slip. He will watch over us. He will keep us from all harm. In all our comings and goings, the Lord will be present to guide, protect, and sustain us. Put your wholehearted trust on that truth.

Today...

Make this psalm your prayerful focus. Declare your allegiance to the Lord. Lift up your eyes to the mountains before you and know that the Lord is by your side to guide, help, and watch over you. Offer your fears to the One who will protect your life day and night, keeping you from all harm both now and forevermore (**Psalm 121**).

I lift up my eyes to the mountains—
where does my help come from?
My help comes from the Lord,
the Maker of heaven and earth.
He will not let your foot slip—
he who watches over you will not slumber;
indeed, he who watches over Israel
will neither slumber nor sleep.
The Lord watches over you—
the Lord is your shade at your right hand;
the sun will not harm you by day,
nor the moon by night.
The Lord will keep you from all harm—
he will watch over your life;
the Lord will watch over your coming and going
both now and forevermore.

As you reflect on the Word, how is God inviting you to pray? What biblical words or phrases are you led to use in your own prayer?

_____

_____

_____

_____

_____

_____

_____

_____

_____

_____

_____

_____

_____

_____

_____

Behold the splendor of the Lord – Believe the promises of his love – Belong to those who unreservedly trust him – Become prayerful in all you are and do.

Day 30

Psalm 139 – How precious to me are your thoughts

The great "omni" Psalm 139 is a powerful declaration of God's omniscience (He is all knowing), omnipresence (He is ever present), and omnipotence (He is all powerful). Verses 1-6 declare his intimate knowledge of you. He knows where you sit and rise. He knows your thoughts and actions. He is familiar with all your ways. He protects and cares for you beyond comprehension. Verses 7-12 remind you that he's with you everywhere – in this present world and in heaven for all eternity. God will offer his hand to guide you in darkness and in light. Verses 13-18 demonstrate his creative love for you, from the time you were in your mother's womb where he knit you together and created your inmost being. All of this is worthy of your praise and adoration, for you are fearfully and wonderfully made. You are precious in his eyes. The vastness of his thoughts of you outnumber the grains of sand along the ocean's edge. Praise the all-knowing, ever-present, all-powerful God. His loving kindness is all-sufficient every day of your life.

Today…

Invite the Lord to search and know your heart. Test your allegiance to him. Quiet your anxious and fearful thoughts. And, if there is anything offensive to God in your heart, ask him to forgive you, remove it completely, and lead you in the everlasting way. Trust the One who knows you intimately to display his presence and power in and through you, for His glory, now and always. Amen and Amen (**Psalm 139**).

You have searched me, Lord,
and you know me.
You know when I sit and when I rise;
you perceive my thoughts from afar.
You discern my going out and my lying down;
you are familiar with all my ways.
Before a word is on my tongue
you, Lord, know it completely.
You hem me in behind and before,
and you lay your hand upon me.
Such knowledge is too wonderful for me,
too lofty for me to attain.
Where can I go from your Spirit?
Where can I flee from your presence?
If I go up to the heavens, you are there;
if I make my bed in the depths, you are there.
If I rise on the wings of the dawn,

if I settle on the far side of the sea,
even there your hand will guide me,
your right hand will hold me fast.
If I say, "Surely the darkness will hide me
and the light become night around me,"
even the darkness will not be dark to you;
the night will shine like the day,
for darkness is as light to you.
For you created my inmost being;
you knit me together in my mother's womb.
I praise you because I am fearfully and wonderfully made;
your works are wonderful,
I know that full well.
My frame was not hidden from you
when I was made in the secret place,
when I was woven together in the depths of the earth.
Your eyes saw my unformed body;
all the days ordained for me were written in your book
before one of them came to be.
How precious to me are your thoughts, God!
How vast is the sum of them!
Were I to count them,
they would outnumber the grains of sand—
when I awake, I am still with you.
If only you, God, would slay the wicked!
Away from me, you who are bloodthirsty!
They speak of you with evil intent;
your adversaries misuse your name.
Do I not hate those who hate you, Lord,

> *and abhor those who are in rebellion against you?*
> *I have nothing but hatred for them;*
> *I count them my enemies.*
> *Search me, God, and know my heart;*
> *test me and know my anxious thoughts.*
> *See if there is any offensive way in me,*
> *and lead me in the way everlasting.*

As you reflect on the Word, how is God inviting you to pray? What biblical words or phrases are you led to use in your own prayer?

_____

_____

_____

_____

_____

_____

_____

_____

_____

_____

_____

_____

_____

_____

Behold the splendor of the Lord – Believe the promises of his love – Belong to those who unreservedly trust him – Become prayerful in all you are and do.

Day 31

Psalm 100 and 150 – Shout for joy – Praise the Lord!

The psalms are songs of the heart that invite our prayers and provide a guide for the with-God life here on earth. They are filled with authentic language that promote honesty and integrity in the soul of the believer. Several of the psalms are shout-outs for help in time of need. Others are laced with pleas for God's intervention. Many are reflections of the heart toward repentance, confession, thanksgiving, and supplication. All are designed to promote the praise of God's people no matter what life may deliver on the doorstep of our souls here on earth.

As we come to the end of our homebound journey, it's fitting that we close with Psalms 100 and 150, which declare praise and provide for us the language of prayer we can utilize in public and private places where we offer our whole selves into the embracing arms of God. Praise and worship the Lord continuously, in all situations and circumstances of life. Your prayers of praise will delight the heart of the Triune God, Father, Son and Holy Spirit.

Today…

Offer your praise to the Lord with gladness of heart. Come to God with your shouts of joy. His greatness and faithfulness is worthy of your adoration. Praise Him for who He is and give thanks for as many of his attributes as possible. No power on earth surpasses his mighty deeds. He alone is King of Kings and Lord of Lords. Praise the Lord. Alleluia! (**Psalms 100 and 150**)

Psalm 100

Shout for joy to the Lord, all the earth.
Worship the Lord with gladness;
come before him with joyful songs.
Know that the Lord is God.
It is he who made us, and we are his;
we are his people, the sheep of his pasture.
Enter his gates with thanksgiving
and his courts with praise;
give thanks to him and praise his name.
For the Lord is good and his love endures forever;
his faithfulness continues through all generations.

Psalm 150

Praise the Lord.
Praise God in his sanctuary;
praise him in his mighty heavens.
Praise him for his acts of power;
praise him for his surpassing greatness.
Praise him with the sounding of the trumpet,
praise him with the harp and lyre,
praise him with timbrel and dancing,
praise him with the strings and pipe,
praise him with the clash of cymbals,
praise him with resounding cymbals.
Let everything that has breath praise the Lord.
Praise the Lord.

As you reflect on the Word, how is God inviting you to pray? What biblical words or phrases are you led to use in your own prayer?

_____

_____

_____

_____

_____

_____

_____

_____

_____

_____

_____

_____

Behold the splendor of the Lord – Believe the promises of his love – Belong to those who unreservedly trust him – Become prayerful in all you are and do.

About the Author

Stephen A. Macchia is the founding president of Leadership Transformations, Inc. (LTI), a ministry focusing on the spiritual formation needs of leaders and the spiritual discernment processes of leadership teams in local church and parachurch ministry settings. In conjunction with his leadership of LTI, he also serves as the director of the Pierce Center for Disciple-Building at Gordon-Conwell Theological Seminary. He is the author of several books, including *Becoming a Healthy Church, Becoming a Healthy Disciple, Becoming A Healthy Team*, and *Crafting A Rule of Life*. Stephen and his wife, Ruth, are the proud parents of Nathan and Rebekah and reside in Lexington, Massachusetts.

For more information about Stephen A. Macchia or
Leadership Transformations, Inc., visit:
www.LeadershipTransformations.org
www.HealthyChurch.net
www.RuleOfLife.com

Other Titles by Stephen A. Macchia

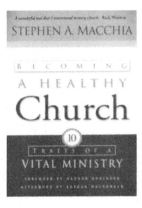

In **Becoming a Healthy Church**, Stephen A. Macchia illustrates how to move beyond church growth to church health. Healthy growth is a process that requires risk taking, lifestyle changes, and ongoing evaluation. This book is a practical, hands-on manual to launch you and your church into a process of positive change. Available in 3 Languages: English, Spanish, Korean.

Becoming a Healthy Disciple explores the ten traits of a healthy disciple, including a vital prayer life, evangelistic outreach, worship, servanthood, and stewardship. He applies to individual Christians the ten characteristics of a healthy church outlined in his previous book, Becoming a Healthy Church. Discipleship is a lifelong apprenticeship to Jesus Christ, the master teacher. Macchia looks to John the beloved disciple as an example of a life lived close to Christ.

Becoming a Healthy Disciple Small Group Study & Worship Guide is a companion to Steve Macchia's book, *Becoming a Healthy Disciple*. This small group guide provides discussion and worship outlines to enrich your study of the ten traits of a healthy disciple. This 12-week small group resource provides a Study, Worship, and Prayer guidelines for each session.

Becoming a Healthy Team is essential for building the kingdom. Stephen A. Macchia offers tried and tested principles and practices to help your leadership team do the same. He'll show you how to Trust, Empower, Assimilate, Manage, and Serve. That spells TEAMS and ultimately success. Filled with scriptural guideposts, Becoming a Healthy Team provides practical answers and pointed questions to keep your team on track and moving ahead.

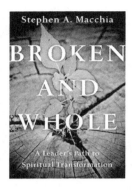

In **Broken and Whole** Stephen A. Macchia offers the gifts of love found in 1 Corinthians 13 as the antidote to our brokenness. He writes with personal transparency from his own experience. Each chapter concludes with a powerful spiritual assessment tool to use in reflecting on our own leadership strengths and weaknesses. By embracing and befriending our own brokenness we can find true wholeness in God's strength. As you progress through the book, you will discover a new way to live in freedom and joy.

In **Crafting a Rule of Life** Stephen A. Macchia looks to St. Benedict as a guide for discovering your own rule of life in community. It is a process that takes time and concerted effort; you must listen to God and discern what he wants you to be and do for his glory. But through the basic disciplines of Scripture, prayer and reflection in a small group context this practical workbook will lead you forward in a journey toward Christlikeness.

Legacy: 60 Life Reflections for the Next Generation will help you capture the wisdom you have gained through years of experiencing the twists and turns of life and record them in a way that makes a great gift for those you love. Not only will they get a window into your heart for them but you might also help them dodge a couple of significant potholes in life. This is a gift that keeps on giving!

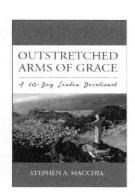

The 40-day Lenten season is typically a time when we choose to abstain from a desire or practice some new measure of devotion. Whether you choose to give something up or take something on (or neither), what's most important is ensuring your heart is attentive to the gifts of grace that Jesus has given by way of his ultimate sacrifice on the cross: forgiveness of sins, fullness of life, and a forever home awaiting for you in heaven. May the journey ahead be good for your soul as you rest in **Outstretched Arms of Grace**.

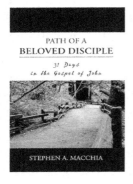

Welcome to the delightful journey of discipleship! Jesus invites us to say an enthusiastic "Yes!" to his beckoning call: Come close, draw near, and follow me. This is exactly what John the Beloved Disciple said long ago and it's our invitation to intimacy today. Becoming a "beloved disciple" of Jesus is the focus of the 31 reflections contained in this devotional guide, **Path of a Beloved Disciple**.

How is your heart condition? In **Wellspring: 31 Days to Whole-Hearted Living** we look at the positive (life-giving) and negative (joy-stealing) conditions of the heart, from both a biblical and relational perspective. With practical applications throughout, this book serves as both a comfort and an inspiration to the reader who longs to reorder their loves for God, his creation, their daily life in God, and their heart for all who cross their path.

Additional Resouces @
SPIRITUALFORMATIONSTORE.COM

Guide to Prayer for All Who Walk With God

The latest from Rueben Job, A Guide to Prayer for All Who Walk With God offers a simple pattern of daily prayer built around weekly themes and organized by the Christian church year. Each week features readings for reflection from such well-known spiritual writers as Francis of Assisi, Teresa of Avila, Dietrich Bonhoeffer, Henri J. M. Nouwen, Sue Monk Kidd, Martin Luther, Julian of Norwich, M. Basil Pennington, Evelyn Underhill, Douglas Steere, and many others.

Guide to Prayer for All Who Seek God
For nearly 20 years, people have turned to the Guide to Prayer series for a daily rhythm of devotion and personal worship. Thousands of readers appreciate the series' simple structure of daily worship, rich spiritual writings, lectionary guidelines, and poignant prayers. Like its predecessors, A Guide to Prayer for All Who Seek God will become a treasured favorite for those hungering for God as the Christian year unfolds.

Guide to Prayer for Ministers and Other Servants
A best-seller for more than a decade! This classic devotional and prayer book includes thematically arranged material for each week of the year as well as themes and schedules for 12 personal retreats. The authors have adopted the following daily format for this prayer book: daily invocations, readings, scripture, reflection, prayers, weekly hymns, benedictions, and printed psalms.

Guide to Prayer for All God's People

A compilation of scripture, prayers and spiritual readings, this inexhaustible resource contains thematically arranged material for each week of the year and for monthly personal retreats. Its contents have made it a sought-after desk reference, a valuable library resource and a cherished companion.

LEADERSHIP
TRANSFORMATIONS INC.

FORMATION | DISCERNMENT | RENEWAL

- Soul Care Retreats and Soul Sabbaths
- Emmaus: Spiritual Leadership Communities
- Selah: Certificate Program in Spiritual Direction (Selah-West, Selah East)
- Spiritual Formation Groups
- Spiritual Health Assessments
- Spiritual Discernment for Teams
- Sabbatical Planning
- Spiritual Formation Resources

Visit www.LeadershipTransformations.org or call (877) TEAM LTI.

Made in the USA
Columbia, SC
17 October 2021

47350161R00095